Florentine™

Lives of the Saints

Saint Gerard

with Prayers and Devotions

I0893805

Regina Press

Nihil Obstat: Reverend Robert O. Morrissey, J.C.D.
Censor librorum
May 14, 2004

Imprimatur: Most Reverend William Murphy
Bishop of Rockville Centre
July 7, 2004

THE REGINA PRESS
10 Hub Drive
Melville, New York 11747
www.reginapress.com

Printed in U.S.A.

ISBN: 9780882717555

Introduction

Throughout its history, the Catholic Church has witnessed men and women of all types who have risen up to become models of Christian life. Some were great preachers, others had extraordinary compassion for God's poor, and still others attained great spiritual maturity. Christians call these special persons saints.

More often than not, however, the saints grew up in rather ordinary circumstances, without any apparently special gifts or talents. Nothing about them hinted at the spiritual and moral greatness they would later achieve.

Thus it was with St. Gerard Majella. He came from a humble family in southern Italy. At the age of twelve, he apprenticed with a man who heaped verbal and physical abuse on him. He enjoyed a moderately successful career as a tailor, but did not particularly distinguish himself. After discovering his call to serve God as a religious, he had to beg the local superior of the Redemptorists to accept him. The superior did so, but only reluctantly. He thought so little of the young man that his recommendation for admittance included his opinion that Gerard would amount to nothing more than "a useless lay brother."

But once Gerard was given the opportunity to serve God in his chosen vocation, his unique gifts emerged for all to see and admire.

Gerard was passionate in discerning his calling from God. He was ever attentive to the will of God in his life, in matters both great and small. He prayed and meditated for years to determine how he should serve God with his life. At the same time, he fervently sought out God's will for him in the ordinary affairs of everyday life.

The young Redemptorist had an uncanny ability to read the hearts of people. On many occasions, he was able to encourage believers to confess sins that had gone unspoken for years. In this way, he helped bring many a Christian to reconciliation with God. Clearly, Gerard understood the inner workings of the human heart, its capacity for both heroic acts of goodness and for evil.

Gerard's special compassion for mothers is well-known. His prayers on behalf of mothers and their unborn children were answered on numerous occasions. Even to this day, countless mothers seek the intercession of St. Gerard for a safe and healthy birth. It is not surprising that many consider St. Gerard to be the patron saint of mothers.

The saints certainly stand out as examples of Christian faith, hope, and love. At the same time, their humble humanity gives us hope that we, too, can find holiness, deeper union with God sainthood.

The Life of St. Gerard

The young man from southern Italy had already experienced rejection three times by the congregation of religious men known as the Capuchins. Then, a group of fifteen Redemptorists came to his village of Muro to preach a mission. As he listened to their stirring words and observed their lifestyle and spirituality, Gerard Majella's emotions quickened. He knew in his heart that God was calling him to become a Redemptorist. Now, if only they would accept him.

He was born on April 6, 1726, in Muro, a small town about fifty miles south of Naples, the youngest of five children of Dominic and Benedetta Majella. He had been so sickly at birth that his parents took him immediately to the church for baptism.

His father, Dominic, a tailor by trade, died when Gerard was twelve, forcing the boy to leave school and go to work. He apprenticed with a tailor who, for no apparent reason, didn't like Gerard, to the point where he heaped verbal and physical abuse on him. Gerard silently accepted this as the will of God for him. The apprenticeship lasted four years, at which time his mother felt Gerard was ready to set up a tailor shop of his own, just like his father.

But Gerard surprised his mother and siblings by announcing that he was going to work for the local bishop of Lacedonia. The bishop was a difficult man to work for, given to angry outbursts and endless nagging. His friends advised Gerard not to take the job.

Still, Gerard accepted it willingly. He endured the bishop's difficult personality, accepting his suffering as part of his calling from God, until the bishop died three years later.

Now nineteen, Gerard returned to Muro, where he set up his own tailor shop. His business was successful, but he didn't make much money. Gerard would set aside enough for his mother and siblings, and then give practically everything else away to the poor.

All this time, Gerard felt he had a vocation to the religious life, and asked to be accepted by the Capuchins. After that, he tried to live for a short time as a hermit. He even earned a part in a Passion play at the cathedral in Muro to demonstrate his desire to imitate Christ.

The mission in Muro in 1749 gave Gerard new

hope. He asked the superior, Father Paul Cafaro, to be admitted to the Redemptorists, but the priest refused. Gerard was so persistent, though, that Father Cafaro advised Benedetta Majella to keep her son locked in his room on the night they were leaving Muro, so he couldn't follow them. She did this, but the next morning she found an empty bed, the window open with bed sheets tied together hanging from it, and a note that read, "I have gone to become a saint."

Gerard caught up with the Redemptorists after a rigorous trek of twelve miles. After his repeated and insistent requests, Father Cafaro gave in. He sent Gerard to the Redemptorist house at Iliceto with this note: "I am sending you a useless lay brother."

The young man fell in love with the way of life of the Redemptorists, and it did not take him long to prove himself to the others. He worked tirelessly as a gardener, sacristan, tailor, porter, cook, carpenter, and clerk. His prayer life was continual, and his obedience to his superiors was flawless. He had a special devotion to the Blessed Sacrament, and would spent hours in prayer before the tabernacle. The man who had been called a "useless lay brother" took his first vows on July 16, 1752.

Gerard spent much of his six years with the Redemptorists traveling with and assisting the missionaries. One of his great gifts was his remarkable ability to discern the inner workings of the human conscience. Often he told people of secret sins they had been too ashamed to confess. As a result, he helped bring many sinners back to God. At this time, people already began referring to him as "wonder worker" and il santo — "the saint."

Another of Gerard's noteworthy ministries was with mothers. On one occasion, as he was leaving the home of the Pirafalo family, who were friends of his, one of the daughters noted that he had forgotten his handkerchief. Gerard told the girl to keep it, and that it would be useful to her someday. Years later, this girl was in danger of death in childbirth. She remembered Gerard's words, and asked for the handkerchief. Almost immediately the danger passed, and she gave birth to a healthy child.

On another occasion, a mother asked for Gerard's prayers when both she and her unborn child were in danger. With Gerard's prayerful help, both mother and child came through the ordeal safely.

His spiritual adviser once asked Gerard to write down what he longed for more than anything else. He wrote: "To love God much; always to be united with God; to do all things for the sake of God; to love everything for God's sake; to suffer much for God. My only business is to do the will of God."

In 1754, Gerard would have to endure a serious test of his reputation and integrity. One of his ministries was to encourage young girls who wanted to enter the convent. He would even secure the dowry for poor girls who otherwise would not be able to enter religious life.

A young woman named Neria Caggiano was one of these girls. She entered the convent at Muro, but was unable to adapt to the religious lifestyle and went home after only three weeks. Neria started to spread false stories about the lives of the nuns, and when the people of Muro refused to believe her, she told false stories about Gerard. She wrote a letter to Alphonsus Liguori, Gerard's superior and the founder of the Redemptorists, accusing Gerard of improprieties with the young daughter of a family at whose house Gerard often stayed on his missionary journeys.

The superior called upon Gerard to answer the accusations. However, he remained silent. The superior had no choice but to impose a severe penance on Gerard. He was forbidden to receive Holy Communion, and allowed no contact with outsiders.

As difficult as it was for him to give up contact with people, not receiving Communion was even more difficult for Gerard. He went so far as to ask to be relieved of the duty of serving Mass, for fear he might try to seize the consecrated host from the priest.

Later Neria, having come down with a serious illness, wrote a letter to Alphonsus Ligouri, in which she confessed that the charges against Gerard were fabricated. Alphonsus was filled with joy at this news, and immediately lifted Gerard's penance. Gerard accepted this reversal of fortune with calm equanimity. He had accepted his punishment as the will of God for him, and now he received his vindication in the same way.

Ill health was a way of life for Gerard, and by 1755 he was overcome by hemorrhaging and dysentery brought on by the austerities of his lifestyle. His death seemed imminent, but his director commanded him to get well, and almost immediately Gerard got better and rejoined the community.

But this cure was only temporary. Before long, Gerard was gravely ill again and began to prepare himself for death. He gave himself over to the will of God, and even hung a sign on his bedroom door: "The will of God is done here, as God wills it and as long as he wills it." He often uttered the prayer: "My God, I wish to die in order to do thy most holy will." Gerard Majella died shortly before midnight on October 15, 1755, at just 29 years of age.

Because of his saintly life, Gerard's death was an occasion of great joy and hope, as well as grief. Thousands came to view the body of "their saint." Miracles attributed to his intercession began to be reported from almost all parts of Italy.

Gerard Majella was beatified by Pope Leo XIII on January 29, 1893. During the beatification process, one witness testified that Gerard was known as il santo dei felice parti — the saint of happy childbirth. He was canonized a saint on December 11, 1904.

Prayers by St. Gerard

The Acts of Love

My God, I intend to love You with as many acts of love as Our Lady and all the blessed spirits have loved You since their creation, and with all the faithful of the earth and with the love with which Jesus Christ bore toward himself and those whom He loved.

To the Holy Trinity

Anytime I catch sight of a cross, or a picture of one of the three divine Persons, or hear them mentioned or at the beginning and end of my actions, I intend to say a 'Glory Be to the Father.'

In Honor of the Most Holy Mary

I have a similar intention of honoring Our Lady and any time I see a woman, I will say a 'Hail Mary' in honor of her purity.

Prayers to St. Gerard

Prayer for Expectant Mothers

Almighty and everlasting God, through the working of the Holy Spirit You prepared the body and soul of the glorious Virgin Mary, Mother of God, to be a worthy dwelling for Your Son. Through the same Holy Spirit, You also sanctified St. John the Baptist before his birth, and now I implore You to hear my humble prayer.

Through the intercession of St. Gerard, I beg and ask You to protect all expectant mothers. Protect also the children You have given them so that they may receive baptism by the help of Your saving hand. Grant also, I ask You, that having lived as good Christians on earth, both mothers and children may one day be united in the everlasting happiness of heaven. Amen.

Prayer to St. Gerard

Great St. Gerard, beloved servant of Jesus Christ, perfect imitator of our meek and humble Savior, and devoted child of the Mother of God, enkindle in my heart one spark of that heavenly charity which glowed in yours and made you a seraph of love.

Glorious St. Gerard, because, like your divine Master, you bore without murmur or complaint the calumnies of wicked people when falsely accused of crime, you have been raised up by God as the patron and protector of expectant mothers. Preserve me in the dangers of motherhood, and shield the child I now bear, that it may be brought safely to the light of day and receive the Sacrament of Baptism. Amen.

Prayer to St. Gerard

Dear Redemptorist saint, model priest and religious, compassionate toward suffering mothers, intercede for this expectant mother. Let her not be misguided like those who are willing to put an end to the life they bear within themselves. Instead let her remain ever conscious that she is privileged to be the instrument through whom God brings another life into the world. Encourage her for the good of her child and the glory of the Lord of life. Amen.

Prayer to St. Gerard for Motherhood

Good St. Gerard, powerful intercessor before the throne of God, wonder-worker of our day, I call upon you and seek your aid. You know that our marriage has not yet been blessed with a child and how much my husband and I desire this gift. Please present our fervent pleas to the Creator of life from whom all parenthood proceeds and ask him to bless us with a child whom we may raise up as his child and heir of heaven. Amen.

Prayer to St. Gerard

Most blessed Trinity, I, your child, thank you for all the gifts and privileges which you granted to St. Gerard, especially for those virtues with which you adorned him on earth and the glory which you now impart to him in heaven. Accomplish your work, O Lord, so that your kingdom may come about on earth. Through his merits in union with those of Jesus and Mary, grant me the blessing for which I ask *(mention request).*

And you, my powerful intercessor, St. Gerard,

always so ready to help those who have recourse to you, pray for me. Come before the throne of divine mercy and do not leave without being heard. To you I confide this important and urgent petition *(mention request)*. Graciously take my cause in hand and do not let me end this prayer without experiencing the effects of your intercession. Amen.

Prayer to St. Gerard for a Mother with a Child

Almighty and everlasting God, through the operation of the Holy Spirit, you prepared the body and soul of the glorious Virgin Mary to be a worthy dwelling place of your divine Son, and sanctified St. John the Baptist while still in his mother's womb; listen to my prayer. Through the intercession of St. Gerard, watch over my child and me and protect us at the time of delivery. May my child receive the saving graces of baptism, lead a Christian life and, together with all the members of our family, attain everlasting happiness in heaven. Amen.

Prayer for a Sick Child

St. Gerard who, like the Savior, loved children so tenderly and by your prayers freed many from disease and even death, look down upon us who are pleading for our sick child. We thank God for the great gift of our son (daughter) and ask him to restore him (her) to health if such be his holy will. This favor we beg of you through your love for all children and mothers. Amen.

Thanksgiving for a Safe Delivery

Good St. Gerard, Patron of Mothers, assist me in thanking God for the great gift of motherhood. During the months of my waiting I learned to call upon you and placed the safety of my child and myself under your powerful protection. The great lesson of your trust in God sustained me; your slogan, "God will provide," became my hope and consolation. Thank God for a healthy and normal baby and my own good health. Help me to prize the great treasure of motherhood and obtain for me from God the help to raise my child as a child of God. In gratitude I will continue to call upon you and will tell mothers about their special patron and friend. Amen.

Prayer for Special Blessings

Almighty and loving Father, I thank You for giving St. Gerard to us as a most appealing model and powerful friend. By his example, he showed us how to love and trust You.

From heaven, You have allowed him to shower many blessings on those who call on him. For Your greater glory and my welfare, please grant me the favors that I ask in his name *(mention request).*

And you, my powerful patron, who have always helped those who prayed to you, intercede for me before the throne of God.

Prostrate yourself before that throne and do not leave it until you have been heard. O good saint, to you I confide my fervent prayers. Graciously accept them and, before the end of these days of prayer, let me experience in some way the effects of your powerful intercession. Amen.

Prayer for Respect for Life

St. Gerard, women the world over have adopted you as their patron in the joys and fears of childbearing. Today we invoke your intercession for the pro-life movement.
Pray that all will look upon human life as a great gift from God to be accepted and loved, not as an unwanted burden to be destroyed. Assist from heaven the efforts of those on earth who are enlisted in the Christlike crusade of promoting the dignity and value of all human life, particularly the unborn. This we ask through Christ, our Lord. Amen.

Novena to St. Gerard

(For nine consecutive days pray nine Hail Marys and the following prayer. If possible celebrate the Sacrament of Reconciliation and receive Communion.)

St. Gerard Majella, humble friar so powerful and so good, God seems to want to pour down on us through your hands the most varied of blessings. Obtain for us the blessing of following better, like you, the will of God, of being more faithful in praying to the Mother of the

Redeemer and, if Providence allows, of being relieved of all our ills. O powerful protector, help of Christian families, strengthen the courage of mothers and preserve the souls and bodies of children.

For the sick, obtain health; for troubled hearts, peace; for guilty souls, pardon; for sinners, conversion; and for young people in search of their way, light about their vocation. For everyone, obtain an increase of generosity in the practice of the evangelical virtues, a constant fidelity to Christ and His Mother, and ultimately perseverance until death in the service of God. Amen.

The Litany of St. Gerard

Lord, have mercy on us.
Christ, have mercy on us.
Lord, have mercy on us.
Christ, hear us.
Christ, graciously hear us.
God, the Father of heaven,
    have mercy on us.
God the Son, Redeemer of the world,
    have mercy on us.

God the Holy Spirit, have mercy on us.
Holy Trinity, one God, have mercy on us.
Holy Mary, Mother of Perpetual Help,
pray for us.
St. Joseph, foster father of Christ,
pray for us.
St. Alphonsus, founder of the Congregation of the Most Holy Redeemer, pray for us.
St. Gerard, endowed with extraordinary blessings from early childhood,
pray for us.
St. Gerard, perfect type of a faithful servant,
pray for us.
St. Gerard, shining example for the laboring classes, pray for us.
St. Gerard, great lover of prayer and work,
pray for us.
St. Gerard, seraphic adorer of the Most Blessed Sacrament, pray for us.
St. Gerard, living image of the crucified Savior, pray for us.
St. Gerard, most devoted to the Immaculate Virgin Mary, pray for us.
St. Gerard, bright mirror of innocence and penance, pray for us.
St. Gerard, admirable model of heroic

obedience, pray for us.
St. Gerard, silent victim of ignominious calumny, pray for us.
St. Gerard, great before God for your deep humility, pray for us.
St. Gerard, truly wise by your childlike simplicity, pray for us.
St. Gerard, supernaturally enlightened in divine mysteries, pray for us.
St. Gerard, solely desirous of pleasing God, pray for us.
St. Gerard, zealous promoter of the conversion of sinners, pray for us.
St. Gerard, wise counselor in the choice of vocation, pray for us.
St. Gerard, enlightened guide in the direction of souls, pray for us.
St. Gerard, kind friend of the poor and distressed, pray for us.
St. Gerard, wonderful protector of unbaptized children, pray for us.
St. Gerard, compassionate intercessor in all our wants, pray for us.
St. Gerard, exalted by God through astonishing miracles, pray for us.
St. Gerard, ornament and glory of the

Redemptorist order, pray for us.
Lamb of God who takes away the sins of the world, spare us, O Lord.
Lamb of God, who takes away the sins of the world, graciously hear us, O Lord.
Lamb of God, who takes away the sins of the world, have mercy on us, O Lord.
Pray for us, St. Gerard, that we may be made worthy of the promises of Christ.

Let us pray. O God, who drew St. Gerard unto yourself from his youth, and conformed him in the image of Your crucified Son; grant, we ask You, that following his example, we may be transformed into the same image, through the same Christ our Lord. Amen.